POWERFUL MEDICINE

FAULTY HEARTS
TRUE SURVIVAL STORIES

SANDRA MARKLE

LERNER PUBLICATIONS COMPANY . MINNEAPOLIS

NOTE FROM THE AUTHOR

This book, in fact the whole Powerful Medicine series, was inspired by an opportunity I had while working on another book, *Rescues*, stories of how people were saved from life-threatening situations. While studying how a heart-lung machine works, I had the chance to suit up and be on the sidelines in the operating room during open-heart surgery. I was impressed with both the surgical team and their equipment. I had to know more!

The books in the Powerful Medicine series are the result of long, exciting detective work that let me talk to amazing, caring physicians, surgeons, and researchers. I also got to know patients who faced some of the worst moments of their lives with determination and courage. I consider all the people you'll meet in the Powerful Medicine series heroes—their stories remarkable. You'll also discover, as I did, how amazing the human body really is.

FOR CURIOUS KIDS EVERYWHERE—THEY'RE THE FUTURE!

ACKNOWLEDGMENTS: The author would like to thank the following people for taking the time to share their expertise: Dr. Raimondo Ascione, Consultant Cardio-thoracic Surgeon, Bristol Heart Institute; Dr. Roberta Bogaev, Medical Director, Heart Failure and Cardiac Transplantation, Texas Heart Institute; Dr. Peter Fitzgerald, Director, Center for Cardiovascular Technology, Stanford University Medical Center; Dr. O. H. Frazier, Surgical Director, Cardiac Transplantation and Director, Cardiovascular Surgical Research, Texas Heart Institute; Dr. James K. Min, Assistant Professor of Medicine, Weill Cornell Medical College; Dr. Alfred Nicolosi, Professor Surgery with the Medical College of Wisconsin and Section Chief, Adult Cardiac Surgery, Froedtert Hospital; Dr. George Noon, Professor of Surgery and Chief of the Division of Transplant Surgery and Assist Devices in the Michael E. DeBakey Department of Surgery at Baylor College of Medicine; Dr. Jeremy Pearson, Associate Medical Director, British Heart Foundation; and Dr. Harsh Singh, chief of Cardiothoracic Surgery at Christchurch Public Hospital. A special thank-you to Skip Jeffery for his loving support during the creative process.

Lerner Publishing Company
A division of Lerner Publishing Group, Inc.
241 First Avenue North
Minneapolis, MN 55401 U.S.A.

Website address: www.lernerbooks.com

Library of Congress Cataloging-in-Publication Data

Markle, Sandra.
    Faulty hearts: true survival stories / by Sandra Markle.
      p.   cm. — (Powerful medicine)
    Includes bibliographical references and index.
    ISBN 978–0–8225–8699–9 (lib. bdg. : alk. paper)
    1. Heart—Juvenile literature. 2. Cardiovascular system—Juvenile literature. 3. Heart—Diseases—Juvenile literature. I. Title.
    QP111.6.M37 2011
    612.1—dc22   2009033980

Manufactured in the United States of America
1 - DP - 7/15/10

CONTENTS

Most of the time, we don't think about how our bodies keep us healthy and active. But when we are hurt, we become very aware of the part that is damaged or not working properly. **One of the key parts of the body is the heart.** In this book, you will find real-life stories of people whose damaged hearts put their lives at risk. The stories also tell how doctors and medical researchers helped them get better. And the stories show how science and technology assist doctors in making such amazing recoveries possible.

HEART ATTACK!

ROBERT WALTON JR. thought he felt tired and coughed a lot because he was recovering from pneumonia, a lung disease. **He ignored these problems until, one day, he couldn't get his breath. He also had stabbing pains in his chest.** Robert dialed 9-1-1, and paramedics rushed him to the hospital in his hometown of Milwaukee, Wisconsin.

AMBULANCE

1312
AMBULANCE

THE HEART IS PART OF THE CIRCULATORY SYSTEM. It pumps blood through blood vessels. This system moves blood through three main areas: the lungs, the heart, and the rest of the body. Blood vessels called arteries carry blood away from the heart into capillaries. The capillaries are so tiny that oxygen and food nutrients in the blood can slip through them to supply the needs of individual cells. Cells are the building blocks of the body. The blood picks up wastes from the cells too. Then the blood flows through more vessels, called veins, which return the blood to the heart.

LUNGS

HEART

ARTERIES

VEINS

As soon as Robert entered the emergency room, the medical team checked his vitals: his heart rate, the sounds of his beating heart, and his blood pressure (how hard the blood is pushing against the walls of the blood vessels). To check his heart rate, a nurse pressed on an artery close to the skin at his wrist. The nurse could feel every time his heart pumped, pushing blood through that artery. This is called a pulse. Counting the number of beats in a minute gave the heart's beating rate. At rest, the normal heart rate for an adult is sixty to eighty beats per minute. But Robert's was beating much faster than normal. His heart was having to work extra hard to push blood throughout his body.

Red blood cells are pushed through arteries, like this one, with each heartbeat.

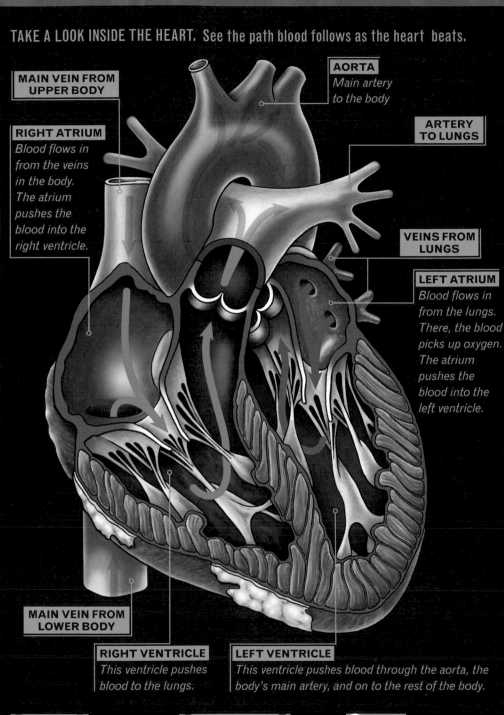

INSIDE THE HEART

TAKE A LOOK INSIDE THE HEART. See the path blood follows as the heart beats.

MAIN VEIN FROM UPPER BODY

AORTA
Main artery to the body

RIGHT ATRIUM
Blood flows in from the veins in the body. The atrium pushes the blood into the right ventricle.

ARTERY TO LUNGS

VEINS FROM LUNGS

LEFT ATRIUM
Blood flows in from the lungs. There, the blood picks up oxygen. The atrium pushes the blood into the left ventricle.

MAIN VEIN FROM LOWER BODY

RIGHT VENTRICLE
This ventricle pushes blood to the lungs.

LEFT VENTRICLE
This ventricle pushes blood through the aorta, the body's main artery, and on to the rest of the body.

ATRIA
Two upper chambers of the heart. They receive blood from the body and push it to the ventricles.

VENTRICLES
Two lower chambers of the heart. They receive blood from the atria and push it out to parts of the body.

VALVE
Flaps that open to let blood pass through and close to keep blood from backing up.

A nurse checked the sound of Robert's heart beating with a stethoscope *(right)*, an instrument that makes sounds louder. A normal heart makes two sounds: *lub dub*.

The lub sound is made when the valves between the atria and the ventricles close. Those valves keep the blood from backing up into the atria. The dub sound is made when the valves between the ventricles and the arteries leading out of the heart close. Those valves keep blood being pushed out of the heart from backing up. Robert's heart made an extra sound—another clue that something was wrong.

This is a healthy aortic valve. The flaps move together when the valve closes.

Next, a nurse checked Robert's blood pressure. The nurse put a kind of cuff around Robert's upper arm and pumped air into it to make it tight. The tight cuff cut off blood flow for an instant. Next, the nurse pressed a stethoscope to Robert's arm just below the cuff. Then he loosened the cuff.

When the nurse heard the blood flowing, he checked the pressure reading on the gauge. This pressure is called systolic pressure. It showed the amount of force Robert's heart exerted when it contracted to pump blood. Next, the nurse used the stethoscope to listen for the changes in heart sounds when Robert's heart relaxed between beats. This is called the diastolic pressure. A blood pressure of 110 to 150 (systolic) over 60 to 80 (diastolic) is normal. Robert's blood pressure was well below normal. There was definitely something wrong with the way his heart was working.

An electrocardiogram (called an EKG, or an ECG) could give more detailed information about Robert's heart. Another member of the medical team attached sensors from the electrocardiograph to Robert's arms, legs, and chest. When the machine was switched on, the sensors sent an electrical signal to the machine each time his heart beat—the stronger the beat the stronger the signal.

The EKG displayed the contractions of Robert's atria and ventricles as a series of spikes—what look like upside-down v's.

The EKG on the top is from a normally beating heart. Robert's results, like the one on the bottom, show an irregular heart rate.

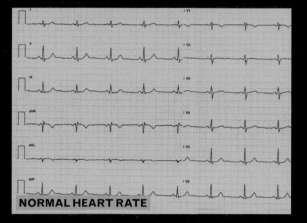

NORMAL HEART RATE

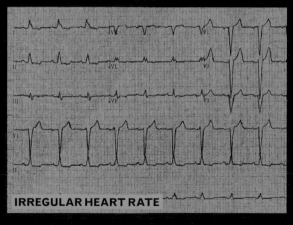

IRREGULAR HEART RATE

His EKG also showed that the problem was happening when his ventricles contracted. It was time to take an X-ray of Robert's heart so his doctor could look at it. An X-ray machine shoots high-energy rays, called X-rays, through the body part being examined.

The technician places a kind of photographic film or a special plate connected to a computer beneath that body part. Wherever X-rays pass through, the area appears dark on the film. Wherever something solid inside the body blocks the X-rays, the area appears white. The X-ray of Robert's chest let his doctors see his heart.

Compare these two X-rays. The one on the left shows a normal heart. Robert's heart, like the one on the right, was much larger than it should be for his body's size. Having an enlarged heart is a disease of the heart muscle.

HEART

Robert's doctor, Dr. Alfred Nicolosi, explained. "Normally, the heart should eject [push out] about sixty percent of the blood that fills it with each beat. But if the heart muscle becomes weak, it may only eject about half the normal amount of blood with each heartbeat. That isn't enough to supply the body's needs. So the heart enlarges in order for the left ventricle to hold more blood and increase the amount flowing out with each of these weaker beats."

But like a balloon getting bigger, enlarging stretches the heart's cells. This makes the heart even weaker than before. Soon the heart is just too weak to work properly.

ENLARGED HEART

To learn how much blood Robert's enlarged heart was pumping with each beat, Dr. Nicolosi ordered a test called an echocardiogram, or echo. This test let the doctor watch Robert's heart in action. A technician placed an instrument that looked like a small flashlight on Robert's chest and aimed it at his heart. The instrument sent out sound waves and picked up the echoes of those sound waves as they bounced off the organs inside Robert's body. A computer converted the echoes into a video. This is one frame from the video of an enlarged heart captured mid-beat.

Dr. Nicolosi said, "Robert's heart was clearly in pretty bad shape because its pumping strength was very weak. That's when our transplant committee met and decided he needed a new heart. He would have to have a heart transplant."

The echocardiogram shows the heart upside down with the ventricle at the top.

But a donor heart wasn't available. Dr. Nicolosi believed Robert was at risk of suffering arrhythmia, a kind of irregular, rapid heart rate that could kill him. If this happened, there might not be time for Robert to get to the hospital. He might not even have time to call for paramedics. So Robert had surgery to install a device called an implantable cardioverter defibrillator (ICD). It was attached to his heart. That way, if Robert's heartbeat became irregular, the ICD would send out an electric charge. And that would immediately jolt his heart back into rhythm. With the ICD making sure that his heart had a regular beat, Robert went home to wait for a donar heart to become available.

Smaller than the smallest cell phone, this defibrillator is a tiny, battery-charged version of the machine hospitals and paramedics use.

Robert said, "I'm lucky Dr. Nicolosi had the foresight to implant the ICD. I felt it fire any number of times—once eleven times in a row."

HEART AT RISK

FOR MARSHALL FITZGERALD, who lives near San Francisco, California, the problem wasn't that his heart was beating irregularly or failing to pump enough blood. It was that he was at risk of having a heart attack. That's because the muscle cells making up his heart weren't receiving enough oxygen-rich blood. **Some of the coronary arteries, the arteries that supply blood to the heart muscle, were partly or completely blocked.** At any time, blood flow to some part of his heart might stop completely. Then he'd have a heart attack. The part of the heart not receiving oxygen stops contracting. If blood flow is cut off long enough, the muscle cells in that area die. **That weakens the heart.**

Marshall went on vacation to Colorado with his family. He thought he would feel better but found he quickly tired just playing with his granddaughter Shannon. He knew something wasn't right.

There are two main coronary arteries, the left and the right. Others branch off from these to reach all parts of the heart muscle.

DR. RAIMONDO ASCIONE IS WORKING ON A WAY TO HELP HEART MUSCLES RECOVER AFTER A HEART ATTACK. First, Dr. Ascione's team collects some of the patient's bone marrow stem cells. These cells usually produce the body's red blood cells. Stem cells are also able to produce copies of whatever kinds of cells are around them. So Dr. Ascione's team injects the stem cells into the heart's damaged muscle. Then they observe how this treatment affects the heart. It will take lots of testing to know for sure if this works. Their hope is that the stem cells will grow into new, healthy muscle cells. These new cells will help the heart work normally again.

This is a section of the left ventricle after a heart attack. The darker part of the muscle has been damaged.

Marshall first knew he had a heart problem because he felt pain in his chest when he exercised. He called his son, Peter Fitzgerald, a doctor who is an expert in treating coronary artery disease. Dr. Fitzgerald arranged for his father's coronary arteries to be examined with a special kind of X-ray machine. It is called a 64-slice CT scanner (computerized tomography scanner). While Marshall rested on a table, a tube that creates X-rays circled around him. As it circled, X-rays directed at his body passed through him. They were picked up by sixty-four detectors that sent signals to a computer.

This is a 64-slice CT scanner. The patient lies on the bed and it slides into the center of the machine.

Dr. James Min explained. "Previous CT scanners only had sixteen detectors. So having sixty-four detectors is like taking a picture of something with lots of cameras instead of only a few. The results are a much more detailed image."

The machine also circles much faster than earlier CT scanners—about three times a second. The images are captured so quickly that breathing and heartbeats don't affect the results.

The image *(right)* shows a normal coronary artery. Compare this to the coronary artery with a blockage *(inset)*. This blockage is similar to Marshall's problem. Normally, a coronary artery is like a tube with an opening as big as a number two pencil. The opening lets blood flow through freely. But plaque, a fatty material that's carried along by the blood, can stick to the inside of the artery walls and narrow the opening.

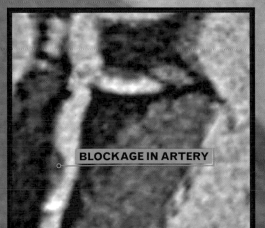

NORMAL CORONARY ARTERY

BLOCKAGE IN ARTERY

Marshall needed a stent to solve his heart problem. A stent is a mesh tube used to flatten the plaque against the artery walls.

Dr. Fitzgerald said, "A stent is inserted—collapsed flat—at the end of a catheter, a long flexible tube. And a live, moving X-ray—fluoroscopy—makes it possible to position the stent inside the coronary artery. Once it is in exactly the right spot, the stent is released, triggering it to open and [press] the plaque against the artery's walls. That lets the blood flow through more freely again."

This stent is inside a coronary artery.

STENT PLUS

THE NEWEST STENTS have the outer surface coated with drugs that stop cells from growing. This prevents the buildup of dense, tough tissue—a scar. Scar tissue could block the artery again.

Dr. Fitzgerald checked his father's partly blocked coronary artery before and after the stent was implanted. He used a machine called an intravascular ultrasound (IVUS). First, he inserted a catheter, a thin, flexible tube, into the main artery of Marshall's leg. The catheter had a miniature sound-producing probe on the end. He threaded it from the leg into the coronary arteries. Sound waves from the probe passed through the blood, struck the artery's walls, and bounced back. A computer picked up and recorded the echoes of these sound waves. It analyzed them and displayed them as an image. The IVUS image on the left below shows the inside of one coronary artery before a stent was implanted. Plaque (colored yellow) is narrowing the artery and limiting blood flow (red). The image on the right shows the same section after a stent was implanted. The plaque is compressed, and the blood flow is much stronger.

Marshall said, "I noticed an immediate improvement. Within a few weeks I was completely back to normal. I feel absolutely great."

PRE-STENT

POST-STENT

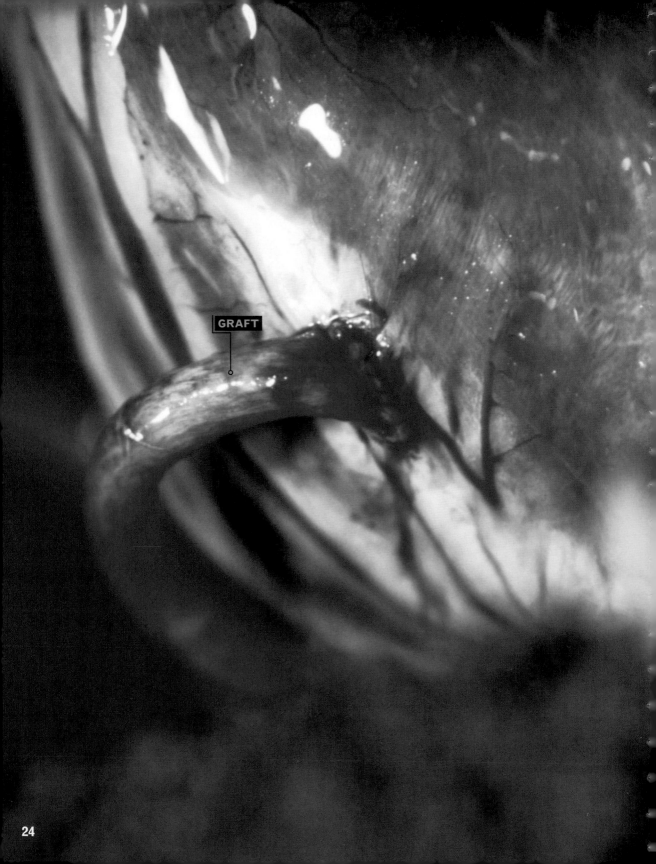

GRAFT

Sometimes part of a coronary artery is completely blocked. Then that section has to be bypassed, or skipped over, for blood flow to be restored to the heart. A bypass is created using a small piece of an artery or vein removed from some other part of the body, such as the leg.

Dr. Harsh Singh explained. "In the past, this surgery was most often performed by opening the chest . . . and stopping the heart. Today, though, this surgery may be performed on a beating heart through just a small incision."

A surgeon cuts open the chest wall to expose the heart. Next, the surgical team collects one piece of blood vessel from another part of the body. This is called a graft. One end is sewn into the coronary artery, just beyond the blockage. The other end is sewn into the aorta, the main artery leaving the heart. That way, blood flows from the artery through the graft to the heart muscle.

GET A GRIP

THIS SPECIAL INSTRUMENT, CALLED THE OCTOPUS, HELPS DOCTORS ATTACH BYPASS GRAFTS TO A BEATING HEART. The octopus got its name from the suction cups on its two prongs. The instrument grips either side of the blocked section of the artery, pulls it up, and holds it still during the surgery.

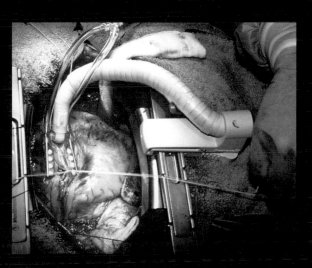

HEART SURGEONS SOMETIMES HAVE THE HELP OF ROBOTS, LIKE THIS ONE. The robot may have three or even four arms. So a surgeon can use many instruments at once. A robot can also handle tinier tools and make smaller motions than a surgeon's hands could manage easily. The surgeon sits at the console, operating the controls with natural hand motions. Then the machine makes the tiny movements needed.

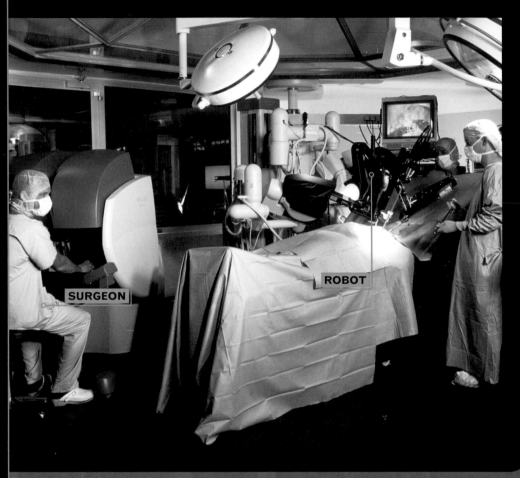

SURGEON

ROBOT

A graft can also help other serious heart problems. One of these is a tear in the lining of the aorta. Doctors call this a dissected aorta. The aorta is the size of a garden hose. Its walls are made of three layers. It is the first artery blood flows through after leaving the heart, so the blood pressure inside it is especially strong. Sometimes, this pressure causes the thin inner layer of the aorta to tear. Then some blood flows through the new pathway between the aorta's torn lining and its middle muscle layer. This new path may cut off the aorta's connection to arteries that branch out to other parts of the body. The aorta could also rupture, or tear open, pouring blood into the body. A dissected aorta needs quick attention. It can be fatal.

AORTA

AORTIC DISSECTION

AORTIC GRAFT

Between 1950 and 1953, Dr. Michael DeBakey invented a new kind of graft especially for repairing torn aortas. It was made of Dacron, a strong fabric. He started by buying 1 yard (about 1 meter) of Dacron and stitching up a test model on a sewing machine. Dacron proved to be ideal for this job. It is sturdy, flexible, and leakproof. The Dacron grafts manufactured at the present time are coated with antibiotics to prevent infection.

In 2005, at the age of ninety-seven, Dr. DeBakey suffered an aortic dissection. Surgeons operated, using the Dacron graft he had invented. This surgery restored his normal blood flow and saved his life.

DURING SURGERIES SUCH AS AORTIC GRAFTS, THE HEART HAS TO STOP BEATING. When it does, the heart-lung machine *(shown below)* takes over the job of supplying the body with oxygen-rich blood. A pump pushes the body's blood into the machine. First, the machine removes the waste carbon dioxide gas from the blood. Then the blood moves into an area where oxygen bubbles through it. The red blood cells pick up oxygen just the way they would in the lungs. A filter removes any air bubbles that could damage the body. Then the machine pumps the blood back into the aorta. From there the blood travels to the rest of the body.

Early in his career, Dr. DeBakey invented a special pump that could move blood without damaging red blood cells. The heart-lung machine was developed using a version of that pump. The heart-lung machine was used during Dr. DeBakey's surgery. So another of his inventions helped to save his life.

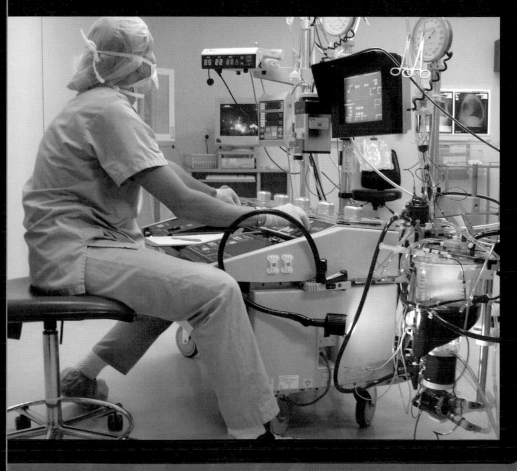

HEART HELPERS

WAITING FOR HIS NEW HEART WAS HARD FOR ROBERT WALTON. He felt tired all the time. His heartbeat was often irregular, so the defibrillator had to reset it. Finally, even that wasn't helping his heart beat normally. He had to go back to the hospital. Robert said, "I told my doctor, 'I don't think I'm going to make it. I think this is the end of the line for me.' "

Dr. Nicolosi said, "Robert wasn't going to live long enough to get a transplant without an LVAD (a left ventricle assist device)."

So Robert was taken to surgery, and doctors implanted an LVAD. The right side of Robert's heart continued to function as usual, but blood flowing into his weak left ventricle continued into the LVAD. There a small electric motor pushed the blood into the aorta. With blood flow once again about normal, **Robert recovered enough to go home and continue waiting for a new heart.**

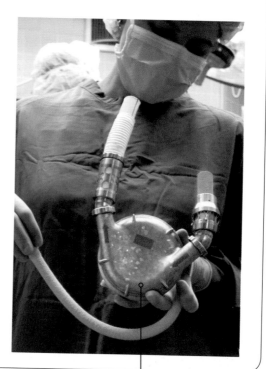

Robert's LVAD was so large it had to be placed inside his abdomen and then attached to his heart.

Robert said, "I needed it, but the LVAD wasn't easy to live with. The two batteries, which I carried around in shoulder harnesses, each weighed about 3 pounds (1.4 kilograms). And they had to be changed about every four hours. It also made a loud *whoosh-whoosh* sound like a washing machine. Anyone within 5 feet [1.5 m] of me could hear it. And that sound—day and night—got irritating."

Shortly after getting his LVAD, Robert celebrated Christmas with his mother Esther Walton. What looks like suspenders on Robert are straps for the LVAD's battery pack.

In Helotes, Texas, Salina Gonzales was also waiting for a new heart. As a teenager, she'd suffered from cancer. Although chemotherapy had cured her, it left her with a weakened heart. She didn't have any symptoms, though, for about ten years. Then, after she recovered from a flulike virus, she started to feel run down. One day, she had trouble breathing. She went to the hospital for help. She was given many of the same tests Robert had been given. The doctors told her that her heart was very enlarged and weakened. They said she probably had less than six months to live unless she received a heart transplant.

Salina said, "I was told, on average, a transplant only gives you ten more years. I wanted more—I wanted a chance to see my little boy, Scott, grow up."

Cardiovascular surgeon Dr. O. H. Frazier implanted the newest model LVAD in Salina's heart. It would give her time to wait for a heart donor. The LVAD was different from the earlier model that kept Robert alive. It was smaller and lighter, and its batteries lasted as long as six hours. It was also a continuous flow pump. As a screw-shaped device turned, it pulled blood in through one end and pushed it out to the aorta at the other end. This kind of pump didn't make a loud swooshing noise. It also pumped a greater amount of blood when Salina was more active. Robert's LVAD always pushed out the same amount of blood whether he was resting or active.

This X-ray shows a newer model LVAD—like the one Salina received.

Salina's cardiologist Dr. Roberta Bogaev said, "The goal was to let Salina's left ventricle rest in the hopes the muscle would recover. At first, the blood went straight through her left ventricle and into the LVAD, which pumped it throughout her body. Her left ventricle didn't pump at all. But, gradually, as Salina exercised and took medication to help strengthen her heart muscle, her left ventricle began to pump again. We were able to turn down the force of the LVAD, letting her heart take over more and more of the work."

Salina said, "Dr. Bogaev told me to try exercising—slowly at first—to see if that would help strengthen my heart. So I did. I went to the gym every day and built up to doing an hour on the treadmill, going as hard as I could. I was determined and full of hope."

At every checkup, Dr. Bogaev reported Salina's heart was getting stronger. On March 12, 2008, seventeen months after it was implanted, the LVAD was removed. Dr. Bogaev said, "A normal left ventricle will squeeze out about 60 percent of the blood that fills it. Salina's left ventricle is pumping out about 40 to 45 percent of the blood. That's not normal, but all things considered, that's very, very good."

Salina and her son, Scott, were thrilled with this news.

REPLACEMENT HEART

ROBERT WALTON'S HEART NEVER IMPROVED. He remained at home, waiting for his new heart. Not just any heart would do, though. It had to be a match.

Dr. Nicolosi explained. "The donor's blood type had to match Robert's. Then the size had to be right. To have the new heart pump properly, you have to put a heart into a patient that comes from a donor who has a similar body size. It's also important that the heart is healthy. So we check if the donor had hepatitis, HIV, cancer, or any of the slow-developing viruses like West Nile virus."

On February 7, 2007—almost two years after the defibrillator was implanted—Robert received the call of his life. A heart donor had died. And the donor was a match for him. That was sad for the donor's family but great news for Robert. He said, "I'd been feeling so depressed. Then the hospital called and told me to be there in forty-five minutes—they had a heart for me. I was suddenly excited and scared at the same time. I wondered if I really was ready for this."

HUMAN BLOOD ISN'T ALL ALIKE. Some people have blood that contains certain proteins and other substances, called antigens. Other people's blood lacks these. So human blood is divided into groups, or types, called A, B, AB, and O. The presence or absence of still other antigens mean each of these types is divided into two groups: those that have it (positive) and those that don't (negative). So, for example, someone with type A blood will have either A+ or A- blood. These blood types affect a person's whole body. So they are critical when someone receives a transfusion, injection of blood, or a transplant of a body part. Receiving the wrong type blood can be fatal. Transplanted body parts from someone with a different blood type will die.

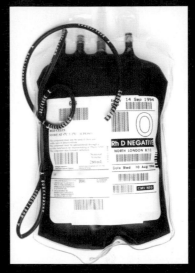

SINCE THE EARLY 1980S, the main way to transport a donor heart had been to inject it with potassium to stop its beating and pack it in ice. The heart could only be kept this way for about four hours, though, before cell death started. A new organ care system *(shown on the right)* has been developed. Once placed in this special transport case, the heart is kept at body temperature. It is also connected to a supply of blood so it can continue pumping. This way the heart stays healthy much longer. That means it can be transported over much greater distances than ever before.

Within hours, Robert's weak heart was being replaced with the donor's strong heart. These are the members of the team that took part in the surgery.

CARDIOVASCULAR SURGEON
The doctor who performed the operation

ANESTHESIOLOGIST
The person who gave anesthesia, a drug to keep the patient unconscious and out of pain.

ASSISTING SURGEON
The doctor who assisted the surgeon during the operation.

CARDIOVASCULAR NURSE
The nurse who handed the surgeon the instruments to be used during the operation.

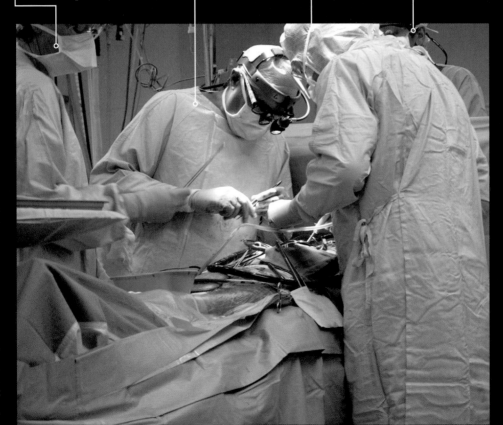

Step One: A surgeon opened Robert's chest. He also cut the pericardium, the sac that covers the heart and the main blood vessels around it. Robert's heart was attached to the heart-lung machine. Surgical instruments, called hemostats, clamped shut the arteries and veins that kept blood flowing through his heart.

The patient is attached to the heart-lung machine.

Then Robert's heart was separated from its main blood vessels.

Step Two: The surgeon removed most of Robert's heart, leaving just the back walls of the right and left atria. The back part of the donor's right and left atria had already been cut away. The surgical team joined the donor heart to Robert's by suturing (stitching) together the halves of the atria.

The donor heart is transplanted into the patient.

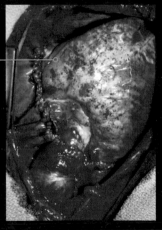

The new heart is given an electric shock to restart it.

Step Three: They attached Robert's main blood vessels to the new heart. The hemostats were removed and blood flowed again. Then Robert's new heart took over pumping blood for his body. He was taken off the heart-lung machine.

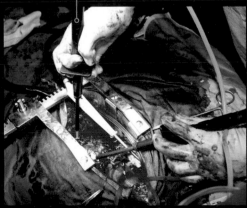

Step Four: Robert's chest was closed and stitched up.

Just a little over two weeks after his surgery, Robert went home. His new life had begun. It included taking care of his new heart. Even though the donor's heart was a good match, it was still foreign to his body. Because of this, his own immune system— organs, tissues, and cells working together to protect the body— would attack it. So Robert had to take medications daily to lessen his body's natural disease-fighting abilities. He also had regular checkups. Fortunately, his new heart remained healthy.

Robert said, "I felt so much better. Best, I felt like I could really breathe again."

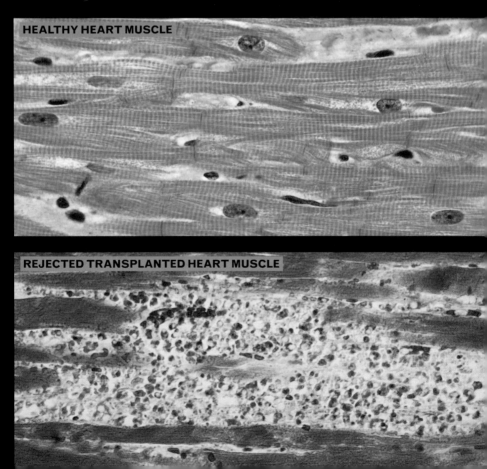

HEALTHY HEART MUSCLE

REJECTED TRANSPLANTED HEART MUSCLE

While most people who receive a heart transplant never know their donor's family, Robert had the chance to meet his donor's grandmother. Robert said, "When we got together, she asked just one thing of me. She asked to put her head on my chest and listen to her granddaughter's heart."

Though the young woman's death had been a tragedy for her family, she'd given Robert the greatest gift anyone can give—a second chance for a healthy life. It's a gift he values every single day.

DR. O.H. FRAZIER IS HEADING A TEAM whose goal is to use the latest technology to develop a permanent replacement heart. In the past, whole artificial hearts have been too big and difficult to live with. Dr. Frazier has developed a thumb-sized pump to help solve the problem of building a heart small enough to fit inside an average-sized chest.

Dr. Frazier said, "There are two major challenges to overcome. First, like a real heart, the right and left side will need to pump with a different amount of force. The right side of the heart only pumps blood to the lungs. The left side pumps blood throughout the body. Secondly, to give people a normal life, the artificial heart will need to be powered from inside the body instead of through wires extending outside to batteries or another power source."

An artificial heart will also need to last for a long time—a lifetime.

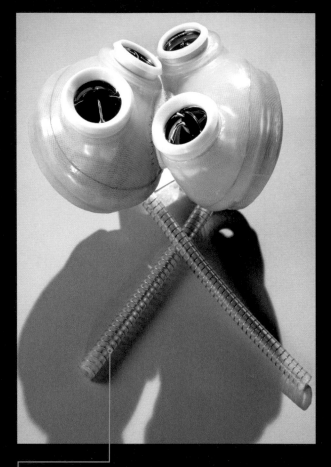

This is the Jarvik-7, an early attempt to build an artificial heart. In 1982, a patient, Barney Clark, survived with a Jarvik-7 for 112 days.

UPDATES

ALTHOUGH MICHAEL DEBAKEY DIED IN 2008, he had lived to be one hundred years old. He lived an active life to the very end. With his new heart, Robert Walton is also very active. He works as a barber, plays basketball, lives on his own, and enjoys time with his family. He leads a full life. So do Salina Gonzales, Marshall Fitzgerald, and the thousands of others who, every year, have their hearts repaired, assisted by a machine, or even replaced by a heart transplant. **Medical research, engineering, and technology make it possible for doctors to mend faulty hearts in ways that could once only be imagined.**

DR. MICHAEL DEBAKEY

ROBERT WALTON

MARSHALL FITZGERALD

SALINA GONZALES

FOR YOUR HEART'S SAKE

- Here are tips for living that will help your heart—and the rest of you—stay healthy.

- Don't smoke. Smokers are twice as likely to suffer a heart attack as nonsmokers.

- Although the recommended daily diet varies with age and lifestyle, the U.S. Food and Drug Administration suggests a diet include plenty of fresh fruits and vegetables. They recommend eating five to nine servings of fruits and vegetables every day. For specific recommendations based on height, weight, age, and activity level, visit: http://www.mypyramid.gov.

- Go easy on salt. Read the labels to check the salt content of foods. Eating a lot of salty foods can cause high blood pressure, which increases the risk of heart disease.

- Walk, ride a bike, swim, or do something else to be active at least thirty minutes every day. Your heart is a muscle, and like all muscles, it needs regular exercise to work at its best.

HEARTS ARE AMAZING!

- The heart beats about 100,000 times a day, pushing blood through a system of vessels about 60,000 miles (96,560 kilometers) long.

- The aorta, the body's largest artery, is about the diameter of a garden hose. Capillaries, the small vessels that connect arteries to veins are only about 1/10 as thick as a human hair.

- In a healthy heart, the left ventricle is about three to four times thicker than the right. That's because the left ventricle has to pump blood much farther and needs more muscle power.

- The average adult man has 5 to 7 quarts (4.7 to 6.6 liters) of blood in his body. An average adult woman has about 1 quart (1 liter) less.

- The heart is in the center of the chest between the lungs. But the bottom of the heart is tipped toward the left side.

GLOSSARY

aorta: the main artery carrying blood away from the heart

arrhythmia: a condition that happens when the heart beats too fast, too slow, or with an irregular pattern

artery: a vessel blood flows through on its way from the heart to the rest of the body

atrium (plural atria): one of the upper chambers of the heart, which receives blood and passes it on to the ventricles

blood: the fluid pumped by the heart. It carries oxygen and nutrients to the body's cells and carries away carbon dioxide and waste. Blood contains plasma (the fluid part of the blood), red blood cells, white blood cells, and platelets.

catheter: a thin, flexible tube for probing or inserting instruments into the body. It is also used to add or remove fluids from the body.

coronary artery: the vessel supplying blood to the heart muscle

echocardiogram: a test that uses sound waves bouncing off the heart to create a moving picture of the heart structure and its functions

electrocardiogram (EKG or ECG): a test that records electrical impulses from the heart as its chambers contract, showing the heart's beating rhythm

heart transplant: the replacement of a damaged or diseased heart with a healthy one

incision: a cut made during surgery

paramedic: a person trained to provide emergency medical care

stent: a device inserted into a narrowed artery to hold it open and increase blood flow

stethoscope: an instrument for listening to the heart's sounds

suture: a stitch used to attach grafts or to close incisions

vein: a vessel that blood flows through when returning to the heart

ventricle: one of the lower chambers of the heart, which pumps out blood

Want to learn more about the heart and the latest medical advancements for treating heart problems? Check these resources.

BOOKS

Bankston, John. *Robert Jarvik and the First Artificial Heart.* Hockessin, DE: Mitchell Lane Publishers, 2002.
Investigate this pioneering step toward a permanently implantable artificial heart.

Brynie, Faith Hickman. *101 Questions about Blood and Circulation: With Answers Straight from the Heart.* Minneapolis: Twenty-First Century, 2001.
These are questions kids really asked with easy-to-understand answers.

Hoffman, Nancy. *Heart Transplants.* Farmington Hills, MI: Lucent Books, 2003.
Read the stories of pioneering surgeons and courageous patients.

Wyckoff, Edwin Brit. *Heart Man: Vivien Thomas, African-American Heart Surgery Pioneer.* Berkeley Heights, NJ: Enslow Elementary, 2007.
This inspiring story is about a man who rose from poverty to become a pioneering heart surgeon and saved countless lives.

WEBSITES

The Franklin Institute: The Human Heart
http://www.fi.edu/learn/heart/index .html
Use the site's tabs to learn more about the heart's structure, function, and tests to monitor heart health. Clicking on highlighted words will let you explore even more.

Mending Broken Hearts
http://ngm.nationalgeographic. com/2007/02/hearts/hearts-interactive
View this narrated slide show of open-heart surgery. Warning: it does contain graphic images some people might find disturbing.

Electric Heart
http://www.pbs.org/wgbh/nova/ eheart/
Kid-friendly animations let you explore how the heart functions and even perform a simulated heart transplant.

SELECTED BIBLIOGRAPHY

BOOKS

National Geographic Society Editors. *Exploring the Human Body: Incredible Voyage.* Washington, DC: National Geographic Society. 1998.

Smeltzer, Suzanne C. and Brenda G. Bare. *Textbook of Medical-Surgical Nursing.* Philadelphia: Lippincott Williams & Wilkins, 2000.

NEWSPAPERS

Berenson, Alex, and Reed Abelson. "The Evidence Gap: Weighing the Costs of a CT Scan's Look Inside the Heart." *New York Times*, June 29, 2008. http://www.nytimes.com/2008/06/29/ business/29scan.html (August 17, 2009).

Jackson, Nancy Beth. "French Research Links Sudden Cardiac Death to Heredity." *New York Times*, April 20, 1999. http://query.nytimes.com/gst/ fullpage.html?sec=health&res=9907 E0DC1F3BF933A15757C0A96F958260 (August 17, 2009).

Nano, Stephanie. "Even Best
Efforts Can't Prevent All Heart
Attacks." *San Francisco Chronicle*,
June 18, 2008. http://www.sfgate.
com/cgi-bin/article.cgi?f=/
n/a/2008/06/18/national/a121820D89.
DTL&hw=stanford&sn=015&sc=183
(August 17, 2009).

WEBSITES

Columbia University Medical Center.
"Cardiac Diseases: Coronary Artery
Disease." *Department of Surgery*. 2009.
http://www.cumc.columbia.edu/dept/
cs/pat/cardiac/chd.html (August 13,
2009).

Felton, Bob. "Replacement Heart
Begins Clinical Trials." *InTech*.
September 2001. http://www.isa.org/
InTechTemplate
.cfm?Section=Article_Index1&t
emplate=ContentManagement/
ContentDisplay
.cfm&ContentID=50286 (August 13,
2009).

The Human Heart. "Monitoring the
Heart." *The Franklin Institute*. N.d http://
www.fi.edu/learn/heart/monitor/
monitor.html (August 13, 2009).

The Medtronic Newsroom. "The
Medtronic Octopus System."
Medtronic. 2009. http://wwwp.
medtronic.com/Newsroom/
LinkedItemDetails.do?itemId=1101864
398829&itemType=backgrounder&lan
g=en_US (August 13, 2009).

University of Chicago Hospital.
"Brilliance 64-Slice CT Scanner by
Philips." *MedGadget*. April 2005. http://
medgadget.com/archives/2005/04/
brilliance_64sl.html (August 13, 2009).

U.S. Department of Health and Human
Services. "Cardiac MRI." *National
Heart, Lung and Blood Institute*. N.d.
http://www.nhlbi.nih.gov/health/dci/
Diseases/mri/mri_show.html (August
13, 2009).

U.S. Department of Health and
Human Services. "How Is Coronary
Angioplasty Done?" *National Heart,
Lung and Blood Institute*. N.d. http://
www.nhlbi.nih.gov/health/dci/
Diseases/Angioplasty/Angioplasty_
howdone.html (August 13, 2009).

TELEPHONE INTERVIEWS

Ascione, Raimondo, M.D., June 19, 2008

Bogaev, Roberta, M.D., July 16, 2008

Fitzgerald, Marshall, July 25, 2008

Fitzgerald, Peter, M.D., June 20, 2008

Frazier, O. H., M.D. June 30, 2008

Gonzales, Salina, June 12, 2008

Hanuschik, Mike, June 14, 2008

Huesman, Tony, June 6, 2008

Min, James, M.D., June 19, 2008

Nicolosi, Alfred, M.D. July 8, 2008

Noon, George, M.D., June 26, 2008

Pearson, Jeremy, M.D., June 20, 2008

Singh, Harsh, M.D., June 16, 2008

Walton, Robert, Jr., June 12, 2008

INDEX

PHOTO CREDITS